IT'S ALWAYS WINE O'CLOCK!

summersdale

IT'S ALWAYS WINE O'CLOCK

An Hachette UK Company
www.hachette.co.uk

Summersdale Publishers Ltd
Part of Octopus Publishing Group Limited
Carmelite House
50 Victoria Embankment
LONDON
EC4Y 0DZ

www.summersdale.com

Printed and bound in the Czech Republic

ISBN: 978-1-78783-008-0

Substantial discounts on bulk quantities of Summersdale books
are available to corporations, professional associations and other
organizations. For details contact general enquiries: telephone:
+44 (0) 1243 771107 or email: enquiries@summersdale.com.

To ....

From ....

WINE GIVES
COURAGE AND
MAKES MEN
MORE APT
FOR PASSION.

OVID

The soft extractive note of an aged cork being withdrawn has the true sound of a man opening his heart.

WILLIAM S. BENWELL

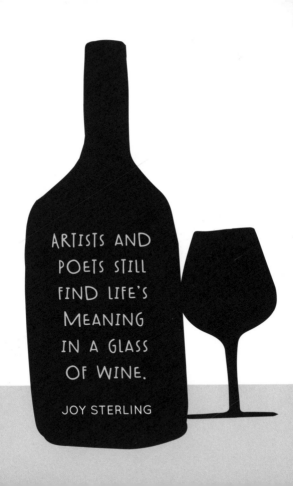

ARTISTS AND
POETS STILL
FIND LIFE'S
MEANING
IN A GLASS
OF WINE.

JOY STERLING

SOBRIETY
DIMINISHES,
DISCRIMINATES,
AND SAYS NO;
DRUNKENNESS
EXPANDS, UNITES
AND SAYS YES.

WILLIAM JAMES

ONE BARREL OF
WINE CAN WORK MORE
MIRACLES
THAN A CHURCH FULL OF
SAINTS.

ITALIAN PROVERB

WINE IS LIFE.

PETRONIUS

AH, DRINK
AGAIN THIS
RIVER THAT IS
THE TAKER-AWAY
OF PAIN, AND
THE GIVER-BACK
OF BEAUTY!

EDNA ST
VINCENT MILLAY

Champagne is appropriate for

BREAKFAST, LUNCH OR DINNER.

MADELINE PUCKETTE

Everybody's got to
believe in something.
I believe I'll have
another drink.

PETER DE VRIES

A WALTZ AND
A GLASS OF
WINE INVITE
AN ENCORE.

JOHANN STRAUSS

Don't put another cup of wine in my hand, pour it in my mouth, for I have lost the way to my mouth.

RUMI

LIKE HUMAN
BEINGS, A
WINE'S TASTE
IS GOING TO DEPEND
A GREAT DEAL ON ITS
ORIGINS AND ITS
UPBRINGING.

LINDA JOHNSON-BELL

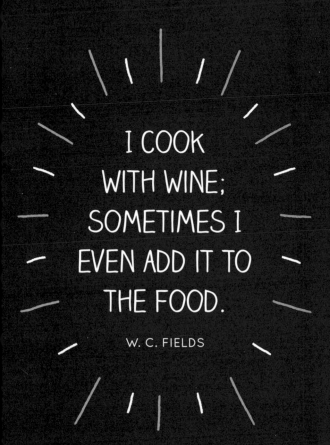

I COOK
WITH WINE;
SOMETIMES I
EVEN ADD IT TO
THE FOOD.

W. C. FIELDS

Wine represents
to me sharing and
good times and a
celebration of life.

DAN AYKROYD

WHENEVER A MAN IS TIRED, WINE IS A GREAT RESTORER OF STRENGTH.

HOMER

I ONLY TAKE A DRINK
ON TWO OCCASIONS
– WHEN I'M THIRSTY
AND WHEN I'M NOT.

BRENDAN BEHAN

A MAN WILL BE
ELOQUENT
IF YOU GIVE HIM
GOOD WINE.

RALPH WALDO EMERSON

WINE IS ONE
OF THE MOST
CIVILIZED THINGS
IN THE WORLD.

ERNEST HEMINGWAY

NOW IS THE
TIME FOR DRINKING,
NOW THE TIME TO
DANCE FOOTLOOSE
UPON THE EARTH.

HORACE

White wine

IS LIKE
ELECTRICITY.

JAMES JOYCE

Too much Chablis
can make you
whablis.

OGDEN NASH

CHAMPAGNE IS
THE CENTREPIECE
FOR THE GREATEST
MOMENTS OF
OUR LIFE.

LAURA DERN

Wine is
bottled
poetry.

ROBERT LOUIS STEVENSON

THE WINE -
IT MADE HER
LIMBS LOOSE
AND
LIQUID.

JODI PICOULT

WINE IS A PASSPORT TO THE WORLD.

THOM ELKJER

Champagne
is one of the
elegant extras
in life.

CHARLES DICKENS

A HANGOVER
IS THE WRATH
OF GRAPES.

DOROTHY
PARKER

A BOTTLE OF WINE
CONTAINS MORE
PHILOSOPHY THAN
ALL THE BOOKS IN
THE WORLD.

LOUIS PASTEUR

WINE ADDS
A SMILE
TO FRIENDSHIP AND
A SPARK
TO LOVE.

EDMONDO DE AMICIS

CHAMPAGNE!
IN VICTORY ONE
DESERVES IT;
IN DEFEAT ONE
NEEDS IT.

NAPOLEON BONAPARTE

WHEN I
DRINK, I THINK;
AND WHEN I
THINK, I DRINK.

FRANCOIS RABELAIS

I only go
to yoga to

DRINK
WINE.

KALEY CUOCO

Drink wine, and you will sleep well. Sleep, and you will not sin. Avoid sin, and you will be saved. Ergo, drink wine and be saved.

GERMAN PROVERB

FOR WHEN THE
WINE IS IN, THE
WIT IS OUT.

THOMAS BECON

Wine is
something that
brings people
together.

DREW BARRYMORE

A BOTTLE
OF WINE
BEGS TO
BE SHARED;
I HAVE NEVER MET
A MISERLY
WINE LOVER.

CLIFTON FADIMAN

GOOD WINE IS
A GOOD FAMILIAR
CREATURE IF IT
BE WELL USED.

WILLIAM SHAKESPEARE

The church is near,
but the road is icy.
The bar is far
away, but I will
walk carefully.

RUSSIAN PROVERB

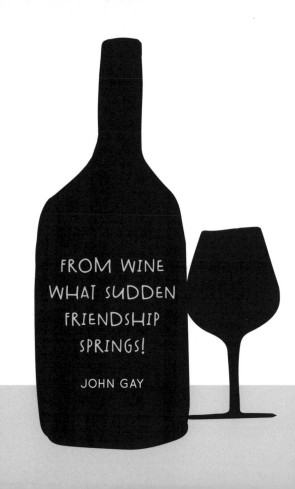

FROM WINE
WHAT SUDDEN
FRIENDSHIP
SPRINGS!

JOHN GAY

WINE CHEERS
THE SAD, REVIVES
THE OLD, INSPIRES
THE YOUNG,
MAKES WEARINESS
FORGET HIS TOIL.

LORD BYRON

A MEAL
WITHOUT
WINE
IS LIKE A
DAY WITHOUT
SUNSHINE.

JEAN ANTHELME BRILLAT-SAVARIN

THERE MUST BE
ALWAYS WINE
AND FELLOWSHIP
OR WE ARE
TRULY LOST.

ANN FAIRBAIRN

WHEN I
READ ABOUT
THE EVILS OF
DRINKING, I GAVE
UP READING.

HENNY YOUNGMAN

Never waste

YOUR WINE.

ELIZABETH
BARRETT BROWNING

Great love
affairs start with
champagne and
end with tisane.

HONORÉ DE BALZAC

THE SHARPER
IS THE BERRY,
THE SWEETER
IS THE WINE.

PROVERB

Just the simple act of tasting a glass of wine is its own event.

DAVID HYDE PIERCE

WINE TO ME IS
PASSION...
WINE IS ART.
IT'S CULTURE.
IT'S THE ESSENCE
OF CIVILIZATION AND
THE ART OF LIVING.

ROBERT MONDAVI

WINE
MEANS THE
RESPONSIBLE
PART OF THE
DAY IS OVER.

JULIE JAMES

There is not the
hundredth part of
the wine consumed
in this kingdom
that there ought
to be. Our foggy
climate wants help.

JANE AUSTEN

DRINK WINE,
NOT LABELS.

MAYNARD
AMERINE

ALCOHOL, TAKEN IN
SUFFICIENT QUANTITIES,
MAY PRODUCE
ALL THE EFFECTS OF
DRUNKENNESS.

OSCAR WILDE

EVERY BOTTLE
HAS A STORY,
AND WHEN YOU
SIT DOWN AND
DRINK IT, YOU FEEL
CONNECTED
TO THAT STORY.

KATE HUDSON

GOOD WINE

PRAISES ITSELF.

DUTCH PROVERB

CHAMPAGNE
IS THE ONE
THING THAT GIVES
ME ZEST WHEN
I AM TIRED.

BRIGITTE BARDOT

All wines should
be tasted; some
should only be
sipped, but
with others,

DRINK THE
WHOLE BOTTLE.

PAULO COELHO

Wine and
friends are a
great blend.

ERNEST HEMINGWAY

MEET ME DOWN
IN THE BAR! WE'LL
DRINK BREAKFAST
TOGETHER.

W. C. FIELDS

Sweet wine
was her element,
and sweet cake
her daily bread.

CHARLOTTE BRONTË

A DRINK
A DAY
KEEPS THE
SHRINK
AWAY.

EDWARD ABBEY

THE FLAVOUR OF WINE IS LIKE DELICATE POETRY.

LOUIS PASTEUR

Sometimes too
much to drink is
barely enough.

MARK TWAIN

AGE AND GLASSES OF WINE SHOULD NEVER BE COUNTED.

ITALIAN PROVERB

WINE IS THE THINKING PERSON'S HEALTH DRINK.

PHILIP NORRIE

I DRINK
WHEN I HAVE
OCCASION,
AND SOMETIMES
WHEN I HAVE
NO OCCASION.

MIGUEL DE CERVANTES

PENICILLIN CURES,
BUT WINE MAKES
PEOPLE HAPPY.

ALEXANDER FLEMING

WINE
REJOICES THE
HEART OF MAN
AND JOY IS THE
MOTHER OF
ALL VIRTUES.

JOHANN WOLFGANG
von GOETHE

The juice of
the grape is
the liquid

QUINTESSENCE
OF CONCENTRATED
SUNBEAMS.

THOMAS LOVE PEACOCK

Fan the sinking flame of hilarity with the wing of friendship; and pass the rosy wine.

CHARLES DICKENS

WHEN A MAN
DRINKS WINE
AT DINNER, HE
BEGINS TO BE
BETTER PLEASED
WITH HIMSELF.

PLATO

Reality is an
illusion created by
a lack of alcohol.

N. F. SIMPSON

WINE IS A
LIVING LIQUID
CONTAINING NO
PRESERVATIVES.

JULIA CHILD

WINE
SPEAKS
TO ALL THE
SENSES.

MARY LOU POSCH

I drink sherry and
wine by myself
because I like it and
I get the sensuous
feeling of indulgence.

SYLVIA PLATH

I RATHER LIKE
BAD WINE;
ONE GETS SO
BORED WITH
GOOD WINE.

BENJAMIN DISRAELI

MY ONLY REGRET
IS THAT I HAVE
NOT DRUNK
MORE CHAMPAGNE
IN MY LIFE.

JOHN MAYNARD KEYNES
ON HIS DEATHBED

THE WORSE
YOU ARE AT
THINKING,
THE BETTER
YOU ARE AT
DRINKING.

TERRY GOODKIND

WINE MAKES DAILY
LIVING EASIER,
LESS HURRIED,
WITH FEWER
TENSIONS AND
MORE TOLERANCE.

BENJAMIN FRANKLIN

IF FOOD
IS THE BODY
OF GOOD
LIVING, WINE
IS ITS SOUL.

CLIFTON FADIMAN

But I'm not
so think as

YOU DRUNK I AM.

J. C. SQUIRE

The great evil
of wine is that
it first seizes
the feet; it is a
crafty wrestler.

PLAUTUS

I NEVER TASTE
THE WINE FIRST
IN RESTAURANTS,
I JUST ASK THE
WAITER TO POUR.

NIGELLA LAWSON

Too much of anything is bad, but too much champagne is just right.

F. SCOTT FITZGERALD

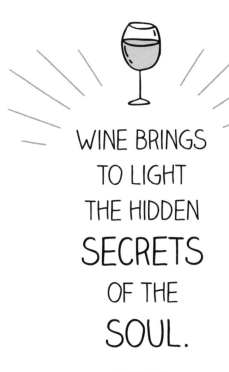

WINE BRINGS
TO LIGHT
THE HIDDEN
SECRETS
OF THE
SOUL.

HORACE

WINE MAKES
A MAN MORE
PLEASED WITH
HIMSELF; I DO NOT
SAY THAT IT MAKES
HIM MORE PLEASING
TO OTHERS.

SAMUEL JOHNSON

I have lived
temperately...
I double the doctor's
recommendation of
a glass and a half
of wine each day
and even treble
it with a friend.

THOMAS JEFFERSON

THE BEST
WINES ARE
THE ONES
WE DRINK
WITH FRIENDS.

ANONYMOUS

THE DISCOVERY OF
A GOOD WINE IS
INCREASINGLY BETTER
FOR MANKIND THAN
THE DISCOVERY
OF A NEW STAR.

LEONARDO DA VINCI

DRINK

IS THE FEAST OF

REASON

AND THE FLOW OF

SOUL.

ALEXANDER POPE

EITHER GIVE ME
MORE WINE OR
LEAVE ME ALONE.

RUMI

A GOURMET
MEAL WITHOUT A
GLASS OF WINE
JUST SEEMS
TRAGIC TO ME
SOMEHOW.

KATHY MATTEA

Wine is
more than
a beverage:

IT'S A
LIFESTYLE.

Wine, taken
in moderation,
makes life, for a
moment, better,
and when the moment
passes life does
not for that reason
become worse.

BERNARD LEVIN

I HAVE TAKEN
MORE OUT
OF ALCOHOL
THAN ALCOHOL
HAS TAKEN
OUT OF ME.

WINSTON CHURCHILL

Three be the things
I shall never attain:
envy, content, and
sufficient champagne.

DOROTHY PARKER

I KNEW I WAS
DRUNK. I FELT
SOPHISTICATED
AND COULDN'T
PRONOUNCE IT.

ANONYMOUS

DRINKING
MAKES
UNINTERESTING
PEOPLE MATTER
LESS AND LATE
AT NIGHT, MATTER
NOT AT ALL.

LILLIAN HELLMAN

Nothing makes the future look so rosy as to **contemplate** it through a glass of Chambertin.

NAPOLEON BONAPARTE

WINE... THE
INTELLECTUAL
PART OF
THE MEAL.

ALEXANDRE
DUMAS

MAN, BEING REASONABLE, MUST GET DRUNK; THE BEST OF LIFE IS BUT INTOXICATION.

LORD BYRON

THE PROBLEM
WITH THE WORLD IS
THAT EVERYONE IS A
FEW DRINKS
BEHIND.

HUMPHREY BOGART

WINE FILLS
THE HEART WITH
COURAGE.

PLATO

AWAY WITH
YOU, WATER,
DESTRUCTION
OF WINE!

CATULLUS

If we sip
the wine, we
find dreams
coming upon us

OUT OF THE
IMMINENT
NIGHT.

D. H. LAWRENCE

Quickly, bring me
a beaker of wine,
so that I may wet
my mind and say
something clever.

ARISTOPHANES

CHAMPAGNE IS THE
ONLY WINE THAT
LEAVES A WOMAN
BEAUTIFUL AFTER
DRINKING IT.

MADAME DE POMPADOUR

Good company, good wine, good welcome, can make good people.

WILLIAM SHAKESPEARE

ABSTAINER:
A WEAK PERSON
WHO YIELDS TO THE
TEMPTATION
OF DENYING HIMSELF A
PLEASURE.

AMBROSE BIERCE

WINE IS A
CONSTANT PROOF
THAT GOD LOVES
US, AND LOVES TO
SEE US HAPPY.

BENJAMIN FRANKLIN

Come quickly,
I am drinking
the stars!

DOM PÉRIGNON

GREAT
WINE WORKS
WONDERS
AND IS
ITSELF ONE.

EDWARD STEINBERG

WINE IS JUST A CONVERSATION WAITING TO HAPPEN.

JESSICA ALTIERI

WINE CAN OF
THEIR WITS THE WISE
BEGUILE,
MAKE THE SAGE
FROLIC
AND THE SERIOUS
SMILE.

HOMER

TIME IS NEVER
WASTED WHEN
YOU'RE WASTED
ALL THE TIME.

CATHERINE
ZANDONELLA

A BOTTLE
OF GOOD WINE,
LIKE A GOOD ACT,
SHINES EVER IN
THE RETROSPECT.

ROBERT LOUIS
STEVENSON

The connoisseur
does not drink

WINE BUT
TASTES OF
ITS SECRETS.

SALVADOR DALÍ

Wine is the
most healthful
and most hygienic
of beverages.

LOUIS PASTEUR

GIVE ME
WINE TO WASH
ME CLEAN OF
THE WEATHER-
STAINS OF CARES.

RALPH WALDO EMERSON

Where there
is no wine there
is no love.

EURIPIDES

WINE IS
EARTH'S ANSWER TO
THE SUN.

MARGARET FULLER

I'D RATHER
HAVE A BOTTLE
IN FRONT OF ME
THAN A FRONTAL
LOBOTOMY.

DOROTHY PARKER

Drinking is a way of ending the day.

ERNEST HEMINGWAY

HEALTH — WHAT
MY FRIENDS
ARE ALWAYS
DRINKING TO
BEFORE THEY
FALL DOWN.

PHYLLIS DILLER

THERE IS A
COMMUNION OF
MORE THAN OUR
BODIES WHEN
BREAD IS BROKEN
AND WINE DRUNK.

M. F. K. FISHER

THIS IS
ONE OF THE
DISADVANTAGES
OF WINE;
IT MAKES A MAN
MISTAKE WORDS
FOR THOUGHTS.

SAMUEL JOHNSON

IN WINE THERE
IS TRUTH.

PLINY THE ELDER

HIS LIPS
DRINK WATER,
BUT HIS HEART
DRINKS WINE.

E. E. CUMMINGS

Within the
bottle's depths,

THE WINE'S
SOUL SANG
ONE NIGHT.

CHARLES BAUDELAIRE

Pour yourself
a drink, put
on some lipstick
and pull yourself
together.

ELIZABETH TAYLOR

MAY OUR LOVE
BE LIKE GOOD
WINE; GROW
STRONGER AS IT
GROWS OLDER.

OLD ENGLISH TOAST

Without bread
and wine, love
goes hungry.

LATIN PROVERB

I BRING AN
UNACCUSTOMED
WINE TO LIPS
LONG PARCHING
NEXT TO MINE, AND
SUMMON THEM
TO DRINK.

EMILY DICKINSON

GOOD WINE IS A NECESSITY OF LIFE FOR ME.

THOMAS JEFFERSON

Burgundy makes you think of silly things, Bordeaux makes you talk of them **and champagne makes you do them.**

JEAN ANTHELME BRILLAT-SAVARIN

WINE IS
PERHAPS THE
CLOSEST THING
THE PLANET HAS
TO AN ELIXIR
OF LIFE.

THOM ELKJER

TO TAKE WINE INTO
OUR MOUTHS IS TO
SAVOUR A DROPLET
OF THE RIVER OF
HUMAN HISTORY.

CLIFTON FADIMAN

WINE CAN BE A
BETTER TEACHER
THAN INK.

STEPHEN FRY

WE ARE ALL
MORTAL UNTIL
THE FIRST KISS
AND THE SECOND
GLASS OF WINE.

EDUARDO GALEANO

THE BIGGER
THE WINE,
THE BIGGER
THE GLASS.

JULIA CHILD

Burgundy
for kings,
champagne
for duchesses,

CLARET FOR
GENTLEMEN.

FRENCH PROVERB

Alcohol is a
misunderstood
vitamin.

P. G. WODEHOUSE

BE CAREFUL TO
TRUST A PERSON
WHO DOES NOT
LIKE WINE.

KARL MARX

Woman first
tempted man to eat;
he took to drinking
of his own accord.

JOHN R. KEMBLE

WINE IS THE
INCARNATION -
IT IS BOTH
DIVINE
AND
HUMAN.

PAUL TILLICH

WINE IS
SUNLIGHT,
HELD TOGETHER
BY WATER.

GALILEO

I feel sorry for people who don't drink. When they wake up in the morning, **that's as good as they're going to feel all day.**

ANONYMOUS

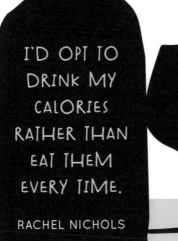

I'D OPT TO DRINK MY CALORIES RATHER THAN EAT THEM EVERY TIME.

RACHEL NICHOLS

HE WHO LOVES NOT
WINE, WOMEN AND
SONG REMAINS A
FOOL HIS WHOLE
LIFE LONG.

MARTIN LUTHER

GIVE ME A
BOWL OF WINE.
IN THIS I BURY ALL
UNKINDNESS.

WILLIAM SHAKESPEARE